Savitri
(Conquest of Death)

OrangeBooks Publication

1st Floor, Rajhans Arcade, Mall Road, Kohka, Bhilai, Chhattisgarh 490020
Website: **www.orangebooks.in**

First Edition, 2025

ISBN: 978-93-6554-889-1

Price: Rs. 196.00

Printed in India

Savitri

CONQUEST OF DEATH

CHIDAMBAR PATIL

OrangeBooks Publication
www.orangebooks.in

Foreword

The conquest of death is a profound theme. Sages, saints, pundits, and scholars have dealt with it since time immemorial. Upanishad karas are the first to see death not as an end but as a transition. Kathopnishat presents a significant dialogue between Nachiketa and Yama, the God of Death. Chanandogya Upanishad focuses on the path of light for those who, possess knowledge, and transcend death. In *the Bhagavad Gita*, Bhagavan Sri Krishna tells Arjuna that the soul is indestructible. Neither weapons can cut it to pieces, nor fire can burn it; neither water can wet it, nor wind can dry it. Of all these, the treatment of death by sage Vyasa is superb. Sage Vyasa is a poet, a seer, and an artist, all rolled into one. He puts the right word in the right place. Hence, the result is—the Savitri Upakhyana in ***The Mahabharata*** emerges as a perfect work of art and philosophy. Throughout the Upakhyana, the emphasis is on the triumph of the radiant soul on dark death.

In English literature too, mystic poets have also contemplated the theme of time, death, and immortality. Wordsworth's message in his *"Intimations of Immortality"* is–that death is not the end of life and that

….The innocent brightness of a new born day
is lovely yet;
The clouds that gather round the setting sun
Do take a sober colouring from an eye
That hath kept watch o'er man's mortality;
Another race hath been and other palms are won…

John Donne, an eminent metaphysical poet, defies death in one of his holy sonnets entitled *"Death Be Not Proud."*

Death, be not proud, though some have called thee
Mighty and dreadful, for thou art not so;
For those whom thou think'st thou dost overthrow
Die not, poor Death, nor yet canst thou kill me…….
……..One short sleep past, we wake eternally
And death shall be no more; Death, thou shalt die.

Prof. C. L. Patil has braved to venture on the path trodden by no less a genius than Sage Vyasa. In our times Sri Aurobindo of Pondicherry has written an epic poem "Savitri" using blank verse, which stands before us as high as the Gourishankar Mountain peak, which no one can equal, let alone surpass. Prof. Patil, too, deserves compliments. His effort reminds me of one statement: 'a man's reach should be higher than his grasp.' Patil employs the quartet containing lines with the end rhyme. He shows his originality in prefacing each Canto with a neat summary, which aids every reader in following the flow of the poem, which deals with the tale of Savitri, a tale of triumph of life over death. It leaves an impression that it is compact and perfect.

This miniature epic has an elaborate Introduction plus 8 Cantos. Canto-I commence with an invocation, invoking ancient sages for inspiration and guidance. The narrative unfolds with the Pandavas in exile, after defeat in the game of dice. They free Draupadi from the clutches of Jayadratha who has abducted her. Then they meet Sage Markandeya, who consoles them. Canto—II recounts the tale of King Ashwapati, in which the divine intervention grants him the boon of a daughter Savitri, whose beauty and virtues make her a paragon of love and virtue. Canto—III narrates Savitri's choice of Satyavana. Savitri is the daughter of the sun, goddess of the supreme Truth and Satyavana is the soul, though divine, yet descending into the grip of death and ignorance. This Canto highlights the interaction of free will and fate, displaying Savitri's courage of conviction and indomitable spirit. Canto—IV captures the union of Savitri and Satyavana, their journey into the forest and Savitri's readiness to face the foreseen trials. The Canto emphasizes the strength of love that transcends materialism and hardship. Savitri becomes the epitome of duty, virtue, and courage. She prepares herself for the unavoidable fulfilment of Sage Narada's prophesy. Canto—V takes us deeper into the crucial day of Satyavana's slipping into Yama's moose, portraying, at the same time, Savitri's commitment to devotion, and her confrontation with Yama. This Canto is a blend of sorrow, strength, and hope. It highlights the inevitability of fate portraying, at the same time, Savitri's spiritual defiance against fate and death. It elevates Savitri to a great height as a beacon light of virtue. Canto—VI continues her remarkable journey towards the ultimate victory over death. She obtains a series of boons and artfully secures her husband's life and blessings for her family, ending in a joyous reunion of Savitri and Satyavana. Canto—VII presents the after-effect of Satyavana's return to life and celebration of Savitri's extraordinary devotion and virtue. This Canto is both celebrative and contemplative. Savitri's tale resonates with the sanctity of love and the deep impact of unwavering devotion. Canto—VIII concludes Savitri's epic journey, celebrating her courage, confidence, and just divine rewards. The tone of this Canto, which is celebratory, conveys the profound message of the conquest of love over death. Savitri's tale is a luminous example of the highest ideals of human life.

Reading this poem was a pleasant treat for me. I am short of words to express my pleasure coming from reading it. The poem, mind-absorbing as it is, is highly enlightening. I admire the courage of Prof. Patil for visiting the tale of Savitri—Satyavana which age cannot wither nor custom stale. May he continue his journey in this realm of gold and enrich it with better works of art. May God Bless him!

Dr. C. R. Yaravintelimath,

Emeritus Professor (Rtd)

Karnataka University, Dharwad.

Authors Confession

This work is inspired by the timeless story of *Savitri and Satyavan* from the *Mahabharata*—a tale as enduring as the stars and as profound as the human soul's journey through love, loss, and triumph. Rooted in the ancient Indian epic, this narrative transcends time, exploring courage, devotion, and the indomitable spirit of the feminine divine. This poem is a labour of love, born from a deep engagement with the *Mahabharata.* Retelling this ancient narrative in poetic form required reverence for the source material and the courage to reimagine its timeless essence in a contemporary voice.

Savitri's story serves as a metaphor for modern women's empowerment. It encourages advocacy for rights, where women stand firm in their beliefs and fight for justice. Leadership involves using intellect and diplomacy to navigate and lead in complex situations. Breaking Stereotypes, challenging societal norms and exercising personal agency. Her narrative transcends its mythological origins, resonating with contemporary efforts to celebrate and empower women in all walks of life.

Savitri, the luminous princess of Madra, defies fate with her stanch will and love for Satyavan, a man fated to die within a year of their union. Through her eloquence and spiritual strength, she confronts Yama, the Lord of

Death, challenging the ultimate adversary and emerging victorious—not through might, but through wisdom, compassion, and the sheer force of her devotion. Her journey is not just the reclamation of her beloved but a profound meditation on the eternal dance between mortality and immortality, human limitation, and divine transcendence.

In this poem, the story of Savitri is retold not as mere mythology, but as a living allegory—a mirror to the human condition. Here, the narrative unfolds with the sweep of an epic and the intimacy of a whispered secret, inviting the reader to traverse landscapes both external and internal: the sylvan beauty of the forest, the sombre stillness of Death's domain, and the luminous realms of the spirit where love reigns supreme.

While writing the poem, though written in quatrains, I sought to remain faithful to the soul of the original, while also weaving into the work a unique sensibility that resonates with modern readers. The crafting of each line has been an act of devotion, balancing the lyrical beauty of the *Mahabharata's* spiritual core with the accessibility of poetic storytelling. The interplay of light and shadow in the narrative—the lush beauty of the forest, the fearful presence of Yama, and the radiant resolve of Savitri—demanded vivid imagery and emotional depth, which I have strived to bring forth with care and diligence.

The journey of creating this poem was one of immersion and introspection. Hours were spent delving into the nuances of the original Sanskrit verses, translated Kannada versions, Aurobindo's *"Savitri"* the cultural and philosophical contexts of the *Mahabharata,* and the universal themes of love, loss, and redemption that make the story eternal. Yet, beyond scholarship, I embraced the story as a living metaphor, allowing its wisdom to seep into the fabric of the verse.

Every stanza reflects my commitment to illuminating Savitri's courage, eloquence, and spiritual grace. The choice of words, rhythm, rhyme, and form was guided by a desire to evoke the grandeur of the epic while infusing it with the intimacy of personal experience. It is a poem not merely written but deeply felt, echoing my grappling with questions of destiny, love, and the triumph of the human spirit.

I offer this work to the readers with the hope that it carries the same light that guided me through its creation—a light that illuminates the path through darkness, just as Savitri's story has for countless generations. To assert, it is a homage not only to Savitri's indomitable will but to the eternal truths embedded in the Mahabharata, which speaks as much to our inner journeys as to the cosmic dramas it portrays.

It will make me happy if this poem obliges as an inspiration to all who seek the courage to face their trials, the wisdom to confront their fears, and the strength to weave love and purpose into the fabric of their lives. In Savitri's story, we are reminded that destiny may write its script, however, it is the human spirit that pens its epilogue.

With profound gratitude, I extend my heartfelt appreciation to all who have played a part in the creation of this poem.

Firstly, to my respected teacher Dr. C. R. Yaravintelimath, Emeritus Professor (Rtd), Karnataka University, Dharwad, who has wholeheartedly come out with a foreword for this poem. His words of wisdom and encouragement have nurtured my poetic voice. Sir, your support has been invaluable. Your insights have refined my words and deepened my understanding of verse and expression.

To my cherished friend, Prof Ramesh Joshi Sir, whose valuable suggestions and guidance have made me feel comfortable in writing the poem. He is one such person who has always found only good things in me. I am grateful to him. And my family, Smt Snehalata, daughters Smt Anusha, Arpita and son Vishal, whose unwavering belief in my craft has been a source of strength—your encouragement, thoughtful critiques, and patient listening have shaped this work in more ways than words can capture.

To the muse, tangible, and intangible, who have stirred my thoughts and inspired my lines, your whispers have given rhythm and meaning to my expressions.

And to every reader who embraces these words, finding within them a reflection of their own emotions, I am deeply humbled by your presence in this journey.

This poem is not merely a solitary creation but a tapestry woven with the kindness, guidance, and inspiration of many. To each of you, I extend my sincerest thanks.

Dr. Chidambar. Patil.

Place: Vijayapura

Introduction

"Deeply embedded in India's spiritual heritage, the theme of conquering death is a central focus in Indian literature, philosophy, and religious writings. It mirrors humanity's timeless pursuit to rise above mortality, achieve moksha (liberation), and grasp the essence of life and death."

In the Indian spiritual tradition, *Spirituality* and *Death* stand as two profound and interwoven concepts. Throughout history, countless individuals have sought—and continue to seek—a deeper understanding of death: its nature, the possibility of transcending it, and what lies beyond. The notion of death, along with the aspiration to conquer or transcend it, forms a central theme in Indian literature, philosophy, and spiritual discourse. These themes are conveyed through rich metaphors, symbolic narratives, and deep philosophical reflections, portraying death not merely as an end but as a natural passage and a powerful gateway to spiritual realisation.

When exploring the theme of death in Indian literature, one naturally turns first to the Upanishads, where death is not portrayed as an end, but as a transition. According to these ancient texts, the soul (*Atman*) is eternal, continuously moving through the cycles of birth and rebirth (*Samsara*). A powerful example appears in the

Kathopanishad, which presents a profound dialogue between Nachiketa, a young spiritual seeker, and Yama, the god of death. Nachiketa earnestly seeks to understand what lies beyond death. In response, Yama imparts a deep spiritual teaching: realising the true self (*Atman*) leads to *Moksha*—liberation that transcends death. He reveals that the *Atman* is eternal, unchanging, and untouched by both birth and death.

"The wise, who realise the self as eternal, formless, all-pervading, and beyond sorrow, transcend death."

(Kathop Upanishad) Chapter 2,
Valli 3, Verse 6 (2.3.6)

Yama says that Liberation (Moksha), as a victory over death, is achieved by realising one's true nature.

"When all desires that cling to the heart fall away, then the mortal becomes immortal and attains Brahman."

(Kathop Upanishad) Chapter 2,
Valli 3, Verse 14 (2.3.14).

The *Chandogya Upanishad* describes two distinct paths after death: the path of light (*Devayana*), followed by those who attain true knowledge and transcend the cycle of rebirth; and the path of smoke (*Pitriyana*), taken by those still bound to *Samsara*, the cycle of birth and death.

In the *Bhagavad Gita*, Krishna reassures Arjuna that the soul is indestructible and beyond harm. Death, he explains, is simply the shedding of the physical body—the eternal *Atman* remains untouched, ever-present, and unchanging.

“For the soul, there is neither birth nor death at any time. It is unborn, eternal, and ever-existing.”

(Bhagavad Gita Chapter 2, (Sankhya Yoga) Verse 20 (2.20))

In Indian mythology and spiritual philosophy, there has long been a profound effort to gain victory over death—*Amritatva*, or immortality. This quest for transcendence is a recurring theme across the Vedas, Puranas, and epics. In these ancient texts, *Amrita*, the nectar of immortality, symbolizes this aspiration. One of the most evocative myths that conveys this struggle is the *Samudra Manthan* (Churning of the Ocean), where gods (*Devas*) and demons (*Asuras*) join forces to churn the cosmic ocean in pursuit of *Amrita*. This allegorical tale represents the eternal human effort to rise above mortality and achieve the divine.

Another path pursued throughout Indian spiritual tradition is the chanting of Vedic hymns—invocations not for physical immortality, but for spiritual liberation. In this context, *immortality* is equated with *Moksha*—the ultimate liberation and the true conquest of death. Moksha represents freedom from the endless cycle of birth and rebirth (*Samsara*), where the soul no longer returns to the world of form and suffering.

In *Advaita Vedanta*, this liberation is understood as the realisation of the unity of *Atman* (the individual self) with *Brahman* (the supreme, all-encompassing reality). In this state of awakened knowledge, death ceases to have any real significance—it is seen as an illusion, a passing shadow before the eternal light of truth.

The Indian epics also explore the mystery of death with philosophical depth. In the *Mahabharata*, the renowned *Yaksha Prashna* episode stands out. Here, Yudhishthira, the eldest Pandava, answers a series of profound questions posed by a divine being—the *Yaksha*. One of the most famous questions is:

"What is the greatest wonder?"

Yudhishthira replies:

"Day after day, countless creatures go to the abode of death, yet those who remain live as though they are immortal. What can be more wondrous than this?"

(Mahabharata, Aranya Parva (Book 3 – The Book of the Forest), Sub-section: Yaksha Prashna or Dharmaraja Samvada, 3.313.116)

This response encapsulates the paradox of human existence: the awareness of mortality, and yet the denial of its immediacy, pointing to the deep-seated human yearning to overcome death not just through belief, but through wisdom and self-realisation.

When Krishna perceives Arjuna's deep moral and emotional dilemma—his reluctance to fight in battle against his kin, teachers, and friends—He begins to guide Arjuna with spiritual wisdom. Krishna explains that the true self, the *Atman*, is eternal, indestructible, and beyond the physical body. The sorrow of killing is misplaced, for the soul neither slays nor can be slain. This teaching marks the beginning of the *Bhagavad Gita's* core philosophical discourse on the nature of life, death, and duty:

"Just as a person discards worn-out clothes and puts on new ones, so does the soul discard a worn-out body and take on a new one."

(the Bhagavad Gita,
Chapter 2, Verse 22, (**2.22**)).

This verse is part of Krishna's teachings to Arjuna on the eternal nature of the soul (*Atman*) and the impermanence of the physical body. Krishna explains that death is an illusion when seen from the standpoint of the eternal *Atman* (Self). The body perishes, but the Self is unchanging and immortal. True victory over death, he teaches, lies not in resisting it but in transcending it through surrender to God and the practice of Bhakti (devotion). By cultivating unwavering devotion, one rises above fear, attains liberation (*Moksha*), and enters a state of eternal peace beyond the cycle of birth and death.

"Whoever remembers Me at the time of death, without doubt, comes to Me."

(the Bhagavad Gita,
Chapter 8 (Akshara Brahma Yoga),
Verse 5, (8.5)).

This verse is central to the Gita's teachings on Bhakti Yoga (the path of devotion), emphasising that remembrance of God at the time of death leads to liberation (*moksha*), which is the true victory over death. This highlights the inevitability of death and the wisdom of preparing oneself for spiritual liberation. Another powerful example appears in the *Shanti Parva* of the *Mahabharata*, where Bhishma—lying on his bed of arrows—demonstrates mastery over death. Endowed with the boon of *icchā-mṛtyu* (the ability to choose the moment of his death), Bhishma postpones his passing until the auspicious time arrives. His self-control and unwavering commitment to *Dharma* exemplify the spiritual maturity required to transcend fear and attachment to mortality.

The *Garuda Purana*, one of the 18 *Mahapuranas* attributed to the sage Vyasa, offers a particularly vivid exploration of death and the afterlife. Named after *Garuda*, the divine vehicle of Lord Vishnu, this *Vaishnavite* text delves into profound metaphysical and ethical questions. It presents a detailed account of the soul's journey after death, the realms it passes through, and the moral consequences of one's actions. Its teachings continue to shape philosophical reflection and encourage a life rooted in dharma and inner awareness.

All these texts, despite their different contexts and styles, converge on a central truth: true victory over death lies in realising the eternal, divine essence within oneself. In Indian spiritual thought, death is not an end but a transformation—a doorway to higher states of being. Overcoming death is not about defying it physically, but about awakening to the imperishable *Self* that exists beyond time and body.

A vivid mythical example of this victory is found in the story of Savitri, a tale of unwavering love, wisdom, and spiritual strength. Narrated by the sage Markandeya in the *Mahabharata*, the story presents Savitri as a woman of great devotion and intellect who successfully confronts *Yama*, the god of death.

When her husband Satyavan dies, Savitri follows Yama as he carries away his soul. Despite Yama's repeated attempts to dissuade her, she persists, engaging him in a profound dialogue about *dharma*, love, and the power of devotion. Impressed by her purity, resolve, and eloquence, Yama grants her three boons—on the condition that she not ask for her husband's life.

Savitri, with great insight, first asks for her father-in-law's lost eyesight and kingdom to be restored. Next, she requests a hundred sons to be born to her and Satyavan. Yama, bound by his word, grants her wishes—only to realise that her second boon cannot be fulfilled without Satyavan's return to life. Realising the cleverness and righteousness of her request, Yama finally relents and restores Satyavan's life.

This episode symbolises not only a triumph over death through devotion and intelligence, but also the empowerment of women in Indian mythology. Savitri's freedom in choosing her husband and her success in reclaiming his life from the god of death reflect her exceptional strength and agency. In essence, her story embodies the ultimate message of Indian spiritual tradition: death may claim the body, but it cannot conquer the soul anchored in truth, love, and righteousness.

The story of Savitri is told in the *Mahabharata* to exemplify the power of a woman's chastity and devotion to her husband and is called 'pativratā māhātmya'. It appears as a minor episode, upākhyāna, in seven sections in Vana Parva, the Book of the Forest of the Great Epic. Rishi Markandeya relates it to exiled Yudhishthira to console him out of his plight of melancholy, distressed as he was by the sufferings of Draupadi; the sage assures him that, in the manner of Savitri, she too will prove a saviour and fortune-bringer to the exiled Pandavas.

King Aswapati of Madra is issueless and performs, for eighteen years, Savitri-Yajna and receives a boon of a radiant daughter from the Goddess. The girl blossoms into full maidenhood in due time, but no noble prince of heroic valour approaches her to claim her hand in marriage. The King advised the Princess to find a husband of her own choice, and she set out on the missioned task, escorted by the elderly counsellors of the Royal Court. Savitri travels to distant lands and visits several ashramas, holy shrines, and gratified capital cities on river banks. She offers her prayers to the deities in pilgrim centres and gives away great charities to the learned and worthy ones as she moves in her pursuit from place to place. Finally, she comes to the deep Shalwa Woods where she meets Satyavan and chooses him as her life partner, as does Satyavan regarding Savitri. Meanwhile, Sage Narad visits Aswapati and returns Savitri to the Palace after accomplishing her mission as they are in conversation. On being queried by her father, Savitri unveils that it is Satyavan whom she has chosen. But instantly Narad, as if to make it firmer, speaks of it as unfortunate; for, Satyavan is fated to die one year after the marriage. Aswapati advises his daughter to make an alternate, but she is unswerving in her resolve. Savitri's choice is made only once and not again. Narad sees and knows that her determination is in conformity with the Dharma and that there is hence a heavenly sanction for it; he blesses the marriage and wishes it to pass off without any mishap. Then Aswapati, following the age-old tradition, makes a formal proposal to Satyavan's father Dyumatsena, and the wedding of Satyavan and Savitri is solemnised in the august presence of the Rishis in the Forest. One year is about to end, and Savitri is greatly afflicted when only four days are left in the life of her husband. She decides to undertake an austere vow of standing at a given place for three days, without taking food. On arrival of that fated day, she worships the Fire God and, after receiving blessings from the elders, accompanies Satyavan to the wood where he must go for his usual work. But, while engaged in the routine work, he suddenly feels tired and begins to sweat profusely. Savitri takes him in her lap and, as foretold by Narad, reckons the coming of the appointed moment. Soon Savitri sees in front of her a dark God snatching the soul of Satyavan and carrying it away with him, even as he starts moving in the southerly direction. Savitri follows him and offers great eulogies to the shining divinity in Yama, and in the process receives several boons from him; finally, she wins back the soul of Satyavan. Returning to the earth the young couple realise that; it has already grown dark in the evening. They resolve to rush and get back to the hermitage where the elders must be waiting for them with all anxiety in their hearts. Dyumatsena is very much disturbed and is appropriately consoled by the wise sages of the ashramas. Then, after the arrival of Satyavan and Savitri, there was great jubilation. On the persistence of Rishi, Gautama Savitri reveals to them several details, beginning with Narad's prophecy of Satyavan's death on that day, Yama's arrival and taking away his soul, and his granting her five boons, including a long life of four hundred years for Satyavan to live with her.

Such is the essential substance of the Mahabharata-Savitri, narrated in 300 ślokas or 600 hemistichs. While the immediate purpose of the poet in giving us the story is to emphasise the power of love and wifely devotion even in the face of death, he goes far beyond the moral, ethical, or religious considerations. The poem is a spiritual document, and the simple episode is a significant proclamation of the inner law in transactions of everyday life. Indeed, the poet suggests that the path of truth-virtue is the path of eternal happiness and salvation. Values that are soul-charged are the only ones which will ultimately prove beneficial in the milieu of worldly affairs as well. Savitri's soul had recognised the truth in Satyavan the moment they met in the Forest, and she clung to it in extremely adverse circumstances too; it was by the power of love that her soul had come out and made the choice, even so much as her nature was ready to accept it as a luminous and infallible guide. She was "driven from within" and, with that force, triumphed over all that stood between her and the sole good she knew by the wonderful alchemy of the newly awakened love in her. The entire thrust of the narrative is on inner perception and the resilience required to abide by it. That is the nature of Satya-Dharma, the Law of Truth, which has always been the sanction of heaven, to walk as well through the peril and disaster of life. Savitri's true greatness is that she upheld it gloriously even in her darkest hour when the mid-day sun stood above her head. Satyavan's death was not an ordinary mortal's death and Yama himself had come on that specified noon to seize his soul. It is in that extraordinariness rose Savitri's indomitable spirit and claimed divinity in the earthly mould giving to it its marvellous glow. To establish this victory, Savitri had prepared herself fully by doing long and difficult Tapasya. She was not only a sizzling princess, kanyā tejasvinī, but was a masterly adept in the Yoga of Meditation, dhyānayogaparāyaṇā, and she was as much proficient in the occult workings too. She alone could affect transformation in the Power of Darkness standing in the way of the supreme event of Love. In giving us such a Savitri the poet himself has climbed extraordinary heights.

The epic is composed and the dignified manner of Vyasa is evident in every line and every description of the upākhyāna. He is austere in the purity of the artistic taste, and there is a complete wholesomeness in its self-sufficient and exact description. Vyasa is too precise a writer to be paraphrased hurriedly. It is a "maturer and nobler work, perfect and restrained in details"—this Savitri-tale, full of vigour, and in reaching its objective directly. Though written in the "morning of his genius", it has already a surer stamp of his Rishihood on it. Assessing the quiet grandeur of its Sri Aurobindo exclaims: "… in the Savitri what a tremendous figure a romantic poet would have made of death, what a passionate struggle between the human being and the master of tears and partings! But Vyasa would have none of this; he had one object, to paint the power of a woman's silent love and he rejected everything which went beyond this or which would have been merely decorative. We cannot regret his choice. There have been plenty of poets who could have given us imaginative and passionate pictures of Love struggling with Death, but there has been only one who could give us a Savitri." It is this story that Sri Aurobindo found charged with the most profound spiritual contents and took it up in its several dimensions to give us his epic of the bright evolutionary fulfilment. The story, though ancient, thus remains ever compelling.

About the symbolic potentials of the Savitri tale, this is what Sri Aurobindo has written: "The tale of Satyavan and Savitri is recited in the Mahabharata as a story of conjugal love conquering death. But this legend is, as shown by many features of the human tale, one of the many symbolic myths of the Vedic cycle. Satyavan is the soul carrying the divine truth of being within itself but descended into the grip of death and ignorance; Savitri is the Divine Word, daughter of the Sun, goddess of the supreme Truth who comes down and is born to save; Aswapati, the Lord of the Horse, her human father, is the Lord of Tapasya, the concentrated energy of spiritual endeavour that helps us to rise from the mortal to the immortal planes; Dyumatsena, Lord of the shining' Hosts, father of Satyavan is the Divine Mind here fallen blind, losing its heavenly kingdom of vision, and through that loss its kingdom of glory. Still, this is not a mere allegory, the characters are not personified qualities, but incarnations or emanations of living and conscious Forces with whom we can enter concrete touch and they take human bodies to help man and show him the way from his mortal state to a divine consciousness and immortal life." Tradition handed down to Vyasa the symbolic myth of the Vedic cycle and he recreated it in the sublimity and splendour of his spiritual attainments; this creation itself has the beauty and form of the damsel of heaven, devarūpinī, to use Vyasa's epithet for Savitri.

Thus, the story of Savitri as a spiritual symbol is the story of the conquest of death by the divine Might incarnate herself in this creation. A supreme moment has arrived in the evolutionary process when such an action is categorically imperative. Man's thousand ills, and all the falsehood enveloping his soul, cannot be redeemed, or removed, and what is there is only the harrowing question lived again and again, interminably. The sacrifices made over the long painful aeons do not seem to appease the Deity seated in the deep heart of the terrestrial darkness. Implacable is the hunger of this enormous shadow-built, rather shadow-assumed, Being and even the gods of heaven are helpless. This cannot be accepted as the eternal fact of existence, and Savitri has come to tackle the issue, tackle it by accepting the load of the death-prone creature, the lot of mortality.

She bore the agony of Satyavan's death, 'duhkham mahān, the great sorrow, and fulfilled the creation in

God. In it is the full implication of Narad's prophecy when he says 'Satyavan must die', and not 'Satyavan will die'; and it is this that renders to the story a certain glowing massiveness to be able to bear the whole weight of spirituality in Sri Aurobindo's *Savitri*.

The death of Satyavan epitomises the travail of earthly existence, and Savitri accepts it to give the solution that lies only in vanquishing the all-devouring Dread present in its fullest proportion in and around us. The certitude is that her action will save the creation—by making the Truth-conscient Light its real guiding sun.

If this is the theme and significance of the Savitri episode, then certainly it is pregnant with the possibility of a new future that can be initiated by the might of the creative Word itself, the mantra. When such a word comes from the highest region, from the causal plane where the speech is Para Vani, transcendental speech, then it brings with it also its effectuating dynamism. The tale is at once a legend and a symbol, a fact of history so old in time that it has become a legend, and a symbol belonging to the occult workings of the affirmative spirituality even in material life. This is what we see in Vyasa's upākhyāna, and in Sri Aurobindo's Epic. Being the creation of a rich Rishihood, each event, each turn of phrase, each verse, sound of word, and sight of image, the entire poetic art including the plot and structure of the poem, everything has the authenticity of expression that comes only from those who are "seers and hearers of the poetic truth and poetic word", kavayah satyaśrutah. That is why it also becomes aesthetically most satisfying and compellingly delightful, needing not one addition or alteration anywhere. Such is the "wonderful poem of faithful Savitri"—if we are to use Winternitz's felicitous phrase.

Unfortunately, however, there is an enormous medievalism that has crept into several narratives of the Savitri tale. It leads not only to confusion and distortion; it also considerably lowers the calm and poised dignity that Vyasa had given to it in his masterly measure. Thus, Romesh Chunder Dutt made the sizzling heroine of the virile poet a feeble and weeping housewife, "taking away the very strength of which she is built", as was pointed out by Sri Aurobindo. It is inconceivable that such an emotional weakling could have triumphed over the strict design of the World and resurrected the soul of her husband, drawing him back from the fearsome jaws of death. There are many small details too that have been added by the later authors, depicting the tastes of their times; but these, instead of enriching the poem, tend to diminish, if not tarnish, its diamond-like perfection, its purity, and coherence. Even to say that a woman can achieve the impossible by the virtue of her chastity, gained through service to her husband, is to moralise the issue and offer a particular brand of social philosophy which cannot satisfy the keenest and deepest instincts of humanity; it becomes, in the strain of a God-fearing religion, an aspect of belief in the efficacy of loyalty which could easily turn out to be a dangerous vital attachment. It is too simplistic and cannot win our admiration on many scores. Certainly, it cannot be the thought of a seer-poet who has the complete power of revelatory expression at his command, and whose vision is always life-ennobling.

Take one or two more examples, the first in the context of Narad's visit to Aswapati. Savitri has returned to the Palace after her discovery and discloses that she has chosen Satyavan for her husband. In one strange version, the heedful father asks the heavenly sage to cast the horoscopes of the young couple and read what the stars foretell about their future; he wants to make sure that the match will be happy. And imagine Narad complying to this request and, after looking at the constellational configuration, announcing the death of Satyavan one year from that day! That would make him blind to his native sight, and bring him down to the level of a village Brahmin astrologer. If the horoscope is to govern the life of this exceptional pair, then there is no doubt that it is the starry destiny, and not Savitri, who is going to gain signal victory over Yama. But the "blithe conjunction of two stars" has another purpose in the spiritual unfolding. If this is not recognised, then it again leads to the same Duttian result—it takes away all the strength the incarnate Goddess had gathered in herself to settle the foreboding dark's issue forever. In yet another version it is also mentioned, without textual support, that Goddess Savitri had not only granted to Aswapati the boon of a son but in her enthusiastic response gave an extra one, of a radiant daughter! Such inanities weaken the force of the narrative, and dim and attenuate the many shades that are there in pristine glory in the original. The Rishi poet has no intention to queer any pitch, or else dramatize or romanticise what is classically solid and tight and most appropriate in every aesthetic and spiritual sense or detail. In it are not the preachings of a moralist, but elevating wisdom and virtue depicting the power of love that can overrule destiny and death.

It is not that the Legend of Savitri is a legend only to the common multitude, and that there is nothing more in it to the illumination. Indeed, it is a very intense and living symbol too, bright and heaven-ascending like the sacrificial fire itself. Its structural framework offers full scope to hold in it spiritual contents of a wide-ranging richness, and its vibrant and gleaming soul benedictive delight in possibilities of the Infinite growing in the earthly life. If the great Sacrifice of the Purusha, the self-renunciation of the Primal Being or, to put it more boldly, his first death, hymned loudly and cheerfully in the Vedas, gave rise to the creation, then it is the supremely forcible Holocaust of Prakriti, of the executive Might, which shall recreate this creation in Divine Body of the Primal Being. That truly seems to be the purpose and significance of Savitri as a Legend and a Symbol is seen transcendentally. The Being's death and then his resurrection by the executive Consciousness-Force to usher in a New World Order in the triple Delight is what is envisaged. And this envisioning has already advanced, and has taken the subtle-physical shape of the Truth-Word, and is now operative in its dynamism to get itself luminously materialised here: the body of the dead Being has already become in evolution sufficiently im-mortal to emerge and breathe the sun-bright intensities of the Super conscience's wonders. Thus, he who is great, mahān, in the world of immortality also becomes great, mahān, in the world of transformed mortality.

For this to be achieved on the human plane, in mṛtyuloka, Satyavan must die; that is the second death of the supreme Being, but now in this creation. In creation, again, it is Savitri who is going to bring the splendours of immortality by removing the death of her spouse. Such are they as incarnate persons amidst us. She, who was silent in the Absolute, has sprung up into action to awaken the one in deathful repose and has accepted the passive role of a witness here. To put it metaphorically in Jnaneshwara's language: "When the Lord goes to sleep the Mistress remains awake and plays herself the part of both." The spiritual-metaphysical Purusha and Prakriti become the tangible and endearing Satyavan and Savitri in human flesh and blood to work out the stupendous alchemy of converting untruth into truth, darkness into light, mortality into immortality.

Prologue

In shadowed forests where fate's breath lingers,
A tale unfolds—of life and death entwined.
Of mortal man and love's immortal fingers,
That weave the threads of destiny divine.

Savitri stands, the dawn's unyielding glow,
A flame against the tempest of the night.
Through paths of sorrow where few dare to go,
She walks with wisdom, faith, and fearless light.

O reader, pause and let these verses guide
Your heart into the depths of truth profound.
For here, amid the ebb and flow of tide,
A timeless whisper in the soul is found.

Come, identify yourself in love's eternal flame—
And find, through Savitri, life's higher aim.

Contents

Canto – I

Invocation For Inspiration

This poem is a reflective and lyrical reiterating of a segment from one of the great Indian epic *Mahabharata*, centring on Draupadi's abduction by Jayadratha and the subsequent events that accentuate themes of virtue, patience, and justice.

The poet begins by invoking sages and deities for inspiration and guidance, emphasising the tale's artistic intent and moral foundation. The narrative unfolds with the Pandavas enduring exile after their defeat in a dice game. While in the forest, Draupadi, resting near a sage's retreat, is approached, and abducted by the lustful Jayadratha. Despite her warnings of dire consequences, he arrogantly persists.

Hearing her cries, the Pandavas chase and subdue Jayadratha. Yudhishthira adhering to Dharma, spares his life for familial ties and compassion, leaving him humiliated and disgraced. Later, the Pandavas encounter the sage Markandeya, to whom Yudhishthira laments Draupadi's unjust suffering. The sage consoles them by sharing wisdom on the certainty of hardships in life, emphasising resilience, patience, and the pursuit of Dharma amidst trials.

The poem balances Draupadi's strength and suffering with the sage's philosophical reflections, encouraging readers to draw lessons on justice, virtue, and perseverance.

To sage Vyasa, my reverent heart inclines,
As I weave this tale from timeless lines.
In storytelling's art, may I unveil,
A poetic fragrance in every tale.

To Ganesha, Shiva-Gowri's cherished heir,
I bow in prayer—may each path be fair.
To Saraswati, goddess of wisdom and grace,
Let words flow sweet, beauty fill this space.

May lovers of art find joy and light,
In these English verses, soft and bright.
I offer this humble song to you,
In hopes each word rings pure and true.

With elders' love and faith as my guide,
Their trust a compass by my side.
May family and kin find joy anew,
In the beauty of this tale, both old and true.

Defeated in the games of dice and chance,
The Pandavas bore their sorrowful stance.
With the fierce maiden by their side,
They entered the forest, their grief to bide.

Through mountains they trekked, enduring the strain,
The years slid by in sorrow and pain.
Ten long years, and yet one more,
Until the awaited event was at their door.

Beneath Kadamba trees near the sage’s retreat,
Sat a beauty with flowing hair, calm and sweet.
Drupada’s daughter, graceful and rare,
Rested there with a noble air.

Jayadratha, lord of Sindhu's land,
With a cruel gaze and bold demand,
His lustful eyes, fierce and sly,
Cast their shadow where she did lie.

He veered from his path, drawn to her grace,
Stopping beside her, face to face.
With eager words, he questioned anew,
"Who are you, fair one? Reveal your truth in words but few."

"I am Draupadi, wife to Pandu’s sons," she declared,
Yet the king, lost in lust, was scarcely spared.
Consumed by desire, with honour tossed,
Shame held no meaning—his line was crossed.

"Evil one, you cannot fathom your doom,
For gazing upon me seals your gloom.
When five valiant warriors rise to defy,
Know that your tale shall wither and die."

"If you wish to keep your life, then bow with grace,
Or your body shall fall, lifeless in this place.
Choose now, for mercy fades with each breath—
Defiance will lead you to certain death."

Heeded not the lady's word, but with pride he strode,
"I am a warrior, a King," he boldly bestowed.
With arrogance and might, he made his claim,
Ignoring her protests, secure in his name.

With her valiant husbands far from near,
The wicked one seized her, disregarding her fear.
He forced her onto his chariot, wild with pride,
And urged his horses, swift in their stride.

The vile man knew not that death drew near,
Unaware of the fate he ought to fear.
Hearing her cries, the five heroes came,
Swiftly to answer, igniting his shame.

With fury rising, they surged behind,
Seizing the wretch, vengeance in mind.
Thrown to the ground, he lay subdued,
As Bhima and Arjuna stood, fierce and renewed.

Seeing Bhima's wrath, Yudhishthira spoke,
"Do not kill him; let mercy not choke.
This is Jayadratha, Dushala's husband, fate-bound to grieve,
Spare him now, for justice will not leave."

"Do not make her a widow; show her some grace,
In the gathering of kin, let compassion take place.
For the righteous understand fate's subtle decree,
And the strength of Dharma, which must always be."

Heeding the brother's words, they left him there,
His body dusted, humbled and bare.
Bruised and shaken, Jayadratha turned away,
A fallen king, his pride in disarray.

Through the forest, they journeyed, trials unending,
Cursing their fate, harsh and unbending.
Pressing onward, they chanced to see,
The sage Markandeya, wise and free.

With reverence, they bowed and took their stand,
Unveiling their woes with hearts unmanned.
Touched by the sage's empathetic gaze,
Yudhishthira spoke, his heart set ablaze.

"My kingdom, my brothers—these hold no fear," he said,
"But Draupadi's suffering fills me with dread.
Why must she endure such torment and pain,
While we are bound by fate's cruel chain?"

"Step by step, with dignity, she bore her sorrow,
This noble woman, in grief's deep furrow.
Has any virtuous soul, in all the world's span,
Endured such trials as she, in fate's cruel plan?"

"Is there one in this world who has suffered as she?
Living with patience, yet bound and unfree.
O sages, will her path forever be dark?
Will no light shine upon her noble heart?"

At the sage's feet, they took their place,
In his presence, a refuge of grace.
With matted locks and prayers unceasing,
The revered sage spoke, his words releasing.

"To those who walk the earth, hardship is near,
Troubles, as natural as life, will appear.
Listen now to tales of the past,
And learn the truths they hold steadfast."

"Many have come, and many have gone,
Bearing their burdens, enduring alone.
Blind to the sorrows that others bear,
Unaware of the weight of shared despair."

“Both waves of joy and sorrow will surge,
Against life's vessel, as it must emerge.
Let each steer their boat with wisdom and care,
Guiding their journey beneath skies so fair.”

"As flowing water seeks the ocean’s shore,
So does life’s journey, yearning for more.
The unfaltering plants, enduring sun and breeze,
Rise strong, withstanding nature’s harsh decrees."

"The moon and stars, behind the clouds, they glide,
Yet in their course, they steadily bide.
Nature’s lesson, clear and wise—
Patience is the root that underlies."

Canto – II

Birth Of Savitri

This canto recounts the tale of King Ashwapati of Madra, his devotion to Dharma, and the divine intervention that grants him the boon of a daughter, Savitri, whose beauty, and virtues make her an ideal of grace and wisdom.

King Ashwapati, though virtuous and beloved, suffers due to his childlessness. Guided by a sage, he performs a sacred sacramental invoking Goddess Savitri, who grants him the boon of a daughter. This act of devotion brings joy and renewal to his lineage.

Savitri is born as a divine blessing, radiant with unmatched beauty and inner virtue. Her presence brings hope and prosperity, and her natural grace surpasses worldly embellishments, making her a symbol of purity and light.

As Savitri grows, her extraordinary qualities intimidate potential suitors, leaving her unmarried despite her father's efforts. This delay becomes a source of concern, reflecting societal pressures on women regarding marriage.

Encouraged by her father, Ashwapati, Savitri takes charge of her destiny, embarking on a journey to find a husband worthy of her virtues. Her determination reflects her strength, autonomy, and adherence to her father's guidance.

Along the way, Savitri demonstrates humility and devotion by offering prayers and charity to sages and ascetics, earning their blessings. Her journey symbolizes the balance of action and faith in navigating life's trials.

The canto concludes with a philosophical reflection on the interplay of joy and sorrow, portraying life as a blend of both. Savitri's story highlights patience, inner strength, and the pursuit of one's path amidst challenges.

"Hear, Yudhishthira, and heed my rhyme,
Of a king's virtue and a woman’s time.
The Madra monarch, noble and wise,
Met fate’s cruel trials beneath dark skies."

"Master of senses, resolute and bright,
Beloved by all, a beacon of light.
Ashwapati, renowned far and wide,
A king of wisdom, his people’s pride."

"Years slipped away, childless and lone,
A life bereft, with sorrow grown.
The scriptures speak, without heirs, life’s strain,
A ceaseless burden, like endless rain."

Seeing his plight, the sage then said,
'Walk the path of Dharma, let your soul be led.
Invoke the sacred, the fire alight,
Through sacrifice, your wish takes flight.'

Adorned in vows, prayed Goddess Savitri with care,
Performing the homa, seeking blessings rare.
From the sacred fire, the goddess did rise,
Pleased with the king, bestowing her prize.

'Hesitate not, O Ashwapati,
Ruler of Madra, with heart so free.
A boon I grant, as your heart aspires,
To fulfil your wish, let your soul catch fire.'

The radiant goddess, divine and bright,
Appeared in the form of unmatched light.
His heart was stirred, his will did sway,
Vows renewed, as night turns to day.

With humble prayer, he sought her grace,
For a lineage true in its rightful place.
Let peace fill hearts and life renew,
In virtue blessed, forever true.

From the queen's grace, a daughter was born,
A gem, like a jewel at the break of dawn.
Amidst the flames, the goddess spoke bright,
Her divine voice, a beacon of light.

At once, she vanished, the goddess withdrew,
Leaving behind peace, her essence anew.
A shiver of grace, her presence still near,
Calm filled the heart, and sorrow disappeared.

By fate's cruel hand, man's toil is sown,
On Earth's harsh soil, his struggles are known.
Yet from the queen's grace, a future did rise,
The dynasty flourished, dispelling the skies.

To fulfil his heart's wish, the king's wealth did grow,
From the moment of vows, blessings began to flow.
In time's fullness, his fate found its rhyme,
With virtuous fruits, his life did shine.

To the royal couple, a daughter was born,
A gem to their hearts, like the dawn of the morn.
With love and devotion, they named her so true,
Savitri, a name that in grace would renew.

With lotus-like eyes and hair flowing dark,
Her face adorned with jasmine's spark.
A nose so delicate, lips soft and sweet,
Teeth that gleam, a beauty complete.

At her sight, doubt turned to resolve,
Her attire transformed, its simplicity dissolved.
Adorned in splendour, radiant and bright,
She glowed with an ethereal, divine light.

Why adorn natural beauty with worldly grace,
When divine radiance beams from her face?
Her inner light, a glow so pure,
Outshines all adornments, as virtues endure.

The daughter grew, blossomed with grace,
And soon came the time for marriage's embrace.
The mother proclaimed, far and wide,
A blissful celebration for all to abide.

The suitors arrived, in awe they stood,
Struck by her grace, as none had ever viewed.
'Are we worthy?' they asked in dismay,
With humbled hearts, they turned away.

People claim shortcomings as fault, ever true,
From then to now, through ages it grew.
For the prince of Madra, much delay did strew,
A heavy setback, with no path in view.

With beauty and virtue, strength in her grace,
Amidst royal grandeur, she found her place.
To hold the hand of her life's true friend,
A wall stood before her, with no means to ascend.

The growing maiden, unmarried, stayed in her home,
A worry for her father, as she continued to roam.
Whispers of judgment, harsh and rife,
Spoke of the delay in the course of her life.

Listen, for patience wanes in worry's flame,
A burning ache, a relentless claim.
The woman who bears life's sorrow and sigh,
Suffers in silence, as time drifts by.

Softly thus spoke Ashwapati, with a heart full of care,
'O princess, seek the one who'll truly share
Your heart's deepest longing, your soul's truest friend,
For love is the journey that has no end.'

'Know your worth, choose wisely,' he said with resolve,
'Hold fast to virtue, let your path evolve.
To the one who values you, pure and true,
I'll grant the wedding, as is just to you.'

She heeded her father's words, setting forth on her quest,
To find her true husband, in her heart a request.
The chariot rolled, through the royal land,
Seeking the man who would take her hand.

Like royal attendants, the ministers did stride,
Following the princess, with watchful eyes wide.
The king's daughter, on her chosen way,
Was shadowed in silence, with respect to sway.

Upon seeing the ascetics in the forest's embrace,
She bowed, her hands folded in humble grace.
With devotion, she gave her charity and prayer,
And in return, received their blessings rare.

She set forth with her heart's longing, seeking her true mate,
Desire burning within, as she faced her fate.
For when the heart's wish is clear, the path may not be seen,
Yet for the one who seeks, it lies in between.

'Hear the truth,' said the sage to the noble prince,
As the tale unfolded, with wisdom so intense.
The wise listened closely, in awe and surprise,
For the story's depths left wonder in their eyes.

With eager hearts, they gathered to hear,
A tale that mingled both joy and fear.
Sweet was the story, yet bittersweet too,
A dance of joy and sorrow in view.

Canto – III

Savitri's Choice Of Satyavana

This canto narrates Savitri's choice of Satyavan as her husband, the portentous prophecy of Sage Narada, and her relentless commitment to love and virtue, even in the face of death.

The wise sage Narada visits King Ashwapati, and Savitri shares the tale of her journey to find Satyavan, a noble soul living in the forest with his exiled, blind father, Dyumatsena. Narada, however, foresees Satyavan's death within a year, casting a shadow over her choice.

Despite her father's pleas to reconsider, Savitri persistently defends her choice. She declares her love for Satyavan and asserts that life's brevity is no reason to abandon virtue, love, or destiny. Her eloquence reflects her wisdom, courage, and strong commitment.

Satyavan is described as the epitome of virtue, embodying strength, humility, and skill. Though his life is fated to be short, his character and actions shine brightly, endearing him to all.

Savitri's reasoning convinces her father, and Narada is moved by her clarity and determination. The sage underlines the inevitability of fate while acclaiming Savitri's wisdom, courage, and devotion, which surpass mere mortal fears.

With the king's consent, Savitri and Satyavan's union is blessed. The canto concludes with a focus on the transcendence of love and virtue over the restraints of time and destiny, symbolising the triumph of moral strength over fear.

This canto highlights the interaction of free will and fate, showcasing Savitri's strength in embracing her path with conviction, even in the face of life's uncertainties.

Once, the wise Narada did appear,
With Mother Earth, he wandered near.
The Madra king, in reverence deep,
Embraced the sage, his joy did leap.

With reverence, he bade the sage to rest,
In humble tones, their greetings blessed.
They spoke of life's ebb, its fickle sway,
And wisdom poured as the sage did say.

The princess returned, her heart alight,
Her face aglow with joy so bright.
Before the sage, with gentle grace,
She bowed, her respects a sweet embrace.

With humble respect, the young girl knelt,
As the sage's blessing on her heart dwelt.
Curious to see her destined skies,
He turned to the king with wise, searching eyes.

Sent forth to seek a groom of grace,
She journeyed far, yet quick her pace.
Ask, if you wish to understand,
The tale of her travels through distant land.

"The king spoke softly, "Daughter, tell,
The story of your quest so well.
Let wisdom's ears now hear and know,
What treasures your journey did bestow."

"I wandered far through lands unknown,
With a longing heart, though so alone.
In a forest glade, my eyes did meet—
There, by fate, our paths did greet."

"His father reigned o'er Sālva's shore,
A noble king, with power to implore.
Yet strife did brew and, in the night,
A rival's hand dimmed Dyumatsena's light."

'Now wanders he, noble Dyumatsena, cast adrift,
With wife and child, through lands that shift.
His sight forsaken by fate's cruel hand,
Yet love's soft guidance helps him stand.'

'His son, Satyavan, noble and true,
Though the kingdom lost, his strength did renew.
In silent penance, with wisdom keen,
He sought out virtues, steadfast and serene.'

‘With humble devotion, he serves his sire,
Bound by duty, his heart’s pure fire.
In him, rare virtues bloom and bind,
A noble soul, in body and mind.’

‘With all my heart, I now confess,
The wishes I hold, both true and blessed.
To you, dear Father, I vow today,
To serve with love, come what may.’

Yet sage Narada, with furrowed brow,
Revealed to the king an error, profound now.
In solemn tones, he spoke of fate,
And the path the princess must navigate.

"Was no other prince worthy of your grace?
Why choose this path, and thus embrace?
An innocent fault, though pure and true,
Yet trials await, as fate will construe."

The king inquired, “Is he not the best?
Has my daughter's choice failed the test?”
‘Yet in my heart, her path feels right,
Though fate may challenge love’s true light.’

When he learned she'd won her desired mate,
The father's heart bowed beneath sorrow's weight.
For who, in this world, can swiftly find
A way to their goal with ease of mind?

In Satyavan shines virtues pure and bright,
A soul of truth, a warrior in might.
Worthy of love, his father's pride,
With strength and honour ever at his side.

Like Rantideva, to charity sworn,
In duty's grace, his soul is reborn.
The sage, with praise, spoke of his might,
For virtues in Satyavan, steady and bright.

One who molds the earth, and tames the steed,
An artist's touch in every deed.
In artistry's realm, unmatched he stands,
"Chitrashva," called by the world's command.

In the forest, with humble grace,
He serves his parents, in that sacred place.
All virtues bloom within his soul,
Yet hidden deep, a flaw takes hold.

Maiden, perhaps you see it not,
But soon the truth will claim its spot.
The sage, with sight beyond mortal veil,
Spoke of a flaw where hopes might pale.

Within a year, his life shall wane,
Death’s shadow looms a destined chain.
Upon these words, the father’s heart
Trembled with fear, as hope did part.

He turned to his daughter with wavering voice,
“Seek another, a safer choice.
For who would wade through death’s dark tide,
Where shadows and poison are known to abide?”

Yet hearing her father’s caution told,
Savitri’s heart grew strong and bold.
“No other love my heart can claim,
For my life is bound to his name.”

For all born on earth, death is a part,
A truth engraved in every heart.
The gift of charity, pure and kind,
Returns to those with a noble mind.

Life may be brief or stretched in span,
Yet worth is found in the heart of man.
Deeds, virtues, and love held fast,
Are treasures beyond what time can last.

When the heart consents, words take flight,
Actions bear fruit, grounded in light.
Wise men speak, when mind is clear,
The path unfolds, beyond all fear.

With wisdom glowing in her eyes,
She spoke of virtue, love's sweet ties.
The sage, his heart moved to see,
The clarity of her noble decree.

For only hearts themselves can feel,
The currents of love, deep and real.
And so, with royal consent, they bind
A vow of duty, heart, and mind.

Fate's hand is etched in time’s embrace,
Hearts may guard secrets in their space.
With reverence, the king did see,
And let their hearts be wise and free.

With words of wisdom, he spoke to the royal line,
And set his gaze towards the heavens, divine.
The sage, with hand raised in peace's embrace,
Offered the king solace, and courage's grace.

In Salva's realm, the king prepared with care,
Ready to meet, with all things fair.
With one heart and mind, Pandavas gathered to hear,
The tale of Savitri, noble and clear.

Canto – IV

Union Of Savitri And Satyavan

This canto captures the union of Savitri and Satyavan, their shared journey into the forest, and the unfolding of Savitri's quiet, resilient strength as she embraces her new life and prepares for the foreseen trials ahead.

King Ashwapati approaches Dyumatsena, the exiled king, with humility and respect, offering his daughter Savitri's hand in marriage to Satyavan. Dyumatsena, despite his hardships, values Ashwapati's honour and accepts the proposal. The dowry is given, but the focus shifts to virtue and character over material wealth.

Savitri's choice to leave behind her life of luxury for the simplicity of the forest is a testament to her virtues and devotion. Her words emphasise that true worth lies in inner grace, not superficial ornamentations.

In her new role, Savitri becomes a symbol of selflessness and care. She earns the love and admiration of her in-laws by accepting her duties with modesty and wisdom, offering emotional and physical support in their struggles.

Despite the joy of her union, the shadow of Satyavan's impending death looms over Savitri. Her silent strength shines as she devotes herself to prayers, vows, and preparations, exemplifying hope, and resilience.

Satyavan's admiration for Savitri grows, as he recognises her unwavering love and virtue. Their bond deepens, both finding consolation and contentment in each other, even as they brace for the trial that destiny may bring.

Canto IV emphasises the strength of character and love that transcends materialism and hardship. Savitri's commitment to her husband and her adaptability to forest life highlight her as an epitome of duty, virtue, and courage. The canto also foreshadows the ultimate test of her love, as she prepares for the eventual fulfillment of Narada's prophecy.

They longed to roam the forest vast,
Where free hearts dwell in peace steadfast;
With wisdom's grace and voices clear,
They pledged their cause, sincere, austere.

The daughters' mates gathered together,
The mother's kin have come near.
On this holy day, with blessings in sight,
The king set forth to the marketplace bright.

In regal grace, the monarch strides,
Where nature's splendour softly abides.
Beneath the banyan's sheltering sprawl,
The cattle pause, content in their thrall.

Greenery whispers, flowers bloom with sacred art,
A hallowed land, a shrine to the heart.
The Madra king, with vision clear,
Beheld the noble sire, revered and near.

With joy, he welcomes them, his heart sincere,
Inquiring softly of their purpose here.
With gentle words, he sought their quest's intent,
Eager to know why to him they were sent.

The daughter's heart, in truth's embrace,
Prayed for her love with hopeful grace.
The sage then spoke, his voice profound,
Revealing the fate the stars had bound.

With love, I honour your son's sweet desire,
And humbly offer my daughter entire.
May their bond endure with joy untold,
A union blessed, in heart and soul.

The state has crumbled, wealth slipped away,
The village distant, into the woods, his path led astray.
What praise remains for a son so bereft,
When fortune has faltered, and light is left.

Raised in comfort, how can she face the wild?
The groom's father speaks with ease, the bride, so mild.
The forest life, so harsh and untamed,
How can a maiden's fate be so framed?

Nature's course is steady, fate's wheel turns with grace,
I see your lineage's pride, its virtues in place.
The greatness of your character shines bold and true,
In the light of your honour, you stand anew.

The truth and love of a father, unfaltering and bright,
Serve as a guide, a beacon of light.
Our hopes seek no ruin, in friendship, we stand,
Bound by respect, love's gentle hand.

Dyumatsena spoke, his thoughts laid bare,
Your open heart knew the wishes we'd share.
Before all, 'O King, our desires were told,
In your wisdom, our hopes took hold.'

With respect, the path was set, the heart's plea voiced,
Yet many turn from those in hardship, their choice.
Distressed, in struggle's grip, few lend their aid,
And many turn away from those who've swayed.

Our love's gift sought, with pride and grace,
The city's princess yearns for the forest's embrace.
Her heart longs for the wild, where freedom flies,
Beyond the city's walls, beneath open skies.

A woman's true worth, not by outward gleam,
But by virtues unspoken, she follows her dream.
In her home, she's a jewel, with honour and grace,
A pride to her land, lighting up its face.

With granted consent, the father beamed,
A joy in his heart, as though in a dream.
In moments of care, with wealth to bestow,
The maiden's dowry, in grace, did glow.

A gem unseen, beyond all quest,
Where gold was found, fate wove the rest.
Satyavan took her hand, so bright,
The Madra king’s daughter, a pure delight.

Satyavan knows, with heart so true,
Savitri was his fortune, his soul’s bright hue.
A husband’s wish, a goddess he gained,
His spirit whisperes fate unchained.

Their boundless love, a secret they shared,
In each other’s hearts, their souls declared.
The forest to them was a heaven’s retreat,
Bound by virtue, their union complete.

The princess cast aside her golden gleam,
Jewels of wealth, no part of her dream.
"Why chase the silks that others adore?
A simple garb holds my worth evermore."

In humble threads, she clad her grace,
To the path of penance, she set her pace.
If women and daughters such wisdom embrace,
Both lineages flourish, blessed in their space.

She stands as grace beneath her husband's shade,
A beacon of love, in her in-laws' aid.
With hands that worshipped and hearts she healed,
Her soul to the forest of humanity appealed.

The sage's words, as Narada spoke,
In the depths of her soul a fire awoke.
A veil of hope, divinely spun,
Guarded her heart like the morning sun.

She counts the days as time drifts by,
In chants, she weaves her silent cry.
With vows like armour, steadfast and bright,
She defies the fates with unwavering light.

Who can discern the heart's deep despair,
As it lingers, unseen, in the earth and air?
Is life but a shadow, serene yet unwise,
When the hour of death hides from our eyes?

The sage's word, enduring, ever true,
A timeless decree, the elders knew.
With grace, they consented, hearts full of care,
And blessed the father, for marriage to share.

In sacred words, her plea did rise,
To shield her love beneath the skies.
Yet the sage's heart, profound and wide,
Eludes the reach of mortal pride.

Satyavan, in silent awe, did see
The devoted wife, steadfast and free.
In truth's pure light, his soul did glow,
A virtuous heart, eternal in flow.

Her heart's deep ache, a secret untold,
Vanished in silence, quiet and cold.
Amidst her thoughts, she sat alone,
Unseen, untouched, with grief unknown.

Canto – V

Satyavana Into Yama's Noose

This canto takes us deeper into the crucial day of Satyavan's death, portraying Savitri's committed devotion, her spiritual strength, and her confrontation with Yama, the god of death. It underscores themes of love, duty, and the triumph of virtue over destiny.

Savitri knowing the destined day approaches, spends three days in intense penance and prayer. Her unwavering devotion astounds her in-laws and the sages, revealing her spiritual strength and purity of purpose. Despite the pleas of her in-laws to rest, Savitri insists on accompanying Satyavan into the forest. Her determination reflects her deep commitment to her sacred vows and to standing beside her husband in the face of destiny.

While engaged in his daily labour, Satyavan is overcome by fatigue and pain. His suffering is vividly described, culminating in his collapse. Savitri's love and care for him remain firm as the moment of fate arrives.

Yama, the god of death, appears in a radiant yet fearsome form, announcing his intent to claim Satyavan's soul. Savitri engages Yama with humility and reverence, seeking to understand his divine role and pleading for her husband's life. Savitri and Yama exchange profound philosophical insights on life, death, and duty. She highlights the virtues of love, compassion, and the sacred bond of marriage, challenging the certainty of death with the strength of her devotion.

Savitri emphasizes that the wife's role is to follow her husband, not only in life but also in death if necessary. Her steadfastness, rooted in love and duty, moves Yama, and exhibits the power of virtue and devotion to transcend even the laws of mortality.

Canto V is a blend of sorrow, strength, and hope. It highlights the inevitability of fate while portraying Savitri's spiritual defiance against it. Her stanch faith and eloquence challenge Yama, setting the stage for a divine resolution.

The canto suggests that true devotion and moral integrity can shape destiny, transforming even the darkest moments into a testament to human strength and divine grace. It elevates Savitri as a beacon of virtue, embodying the power of unwavering faith and love.

The wheel of time rolled swiftly by,
Three days remained 'neath the fleeting sky.
Beyond the morrow, death did wait,
For Satyavan's life, the hand of fate.

Three nights of vigil she steadfastly kept,
With vows unbroken and oaths adept.
Untiring, unfaltering, serene in her way,
In prayer and fasting, her heart did stay.

The father-in-law, with concern, inquired,
"Why such hardship, what has inspired?"
"This vow is mine, for the gods I adore,
No burden it seems," she said, and no more.

"Why should I hinder your sacred vow,
Or cast a shadow upon your brow?
May your devotion reach its crest,
Your joy in faith shall be my rest."

The people marvelled at her penance deep,
In awe, they stood, their voices steep.
The elders, seeing her radiant grace,
Were humbled, silent, in her sacred space.

In the forest's heart, the sages came,
And sat in silence, their spirits aflame.
She bowed in reverence, her prayers to weave,
Honouring elders, their blessings to receive.

The three days waned in devotion true,
The maiden's spirit, steadfast through.
In her penance, a sacred light did shine,
And women beheld, in awe, divine.

They understood that the vow's true might
Resides in the heart, steadfast and bright.
For woman is power, in form and grace,
Her spirit a testament, time can't erase.

"Complete your vow, O noble one," they said,
"To your mother-in-law, the sacred path is led."
In quiet grace, she humbly replied,
"The glory of the vow is mine, with heart open wide."

Today, that fateful day has come,
A storm within, my heart beats like a drum.
Why it arrived, and how it did stay,
The tempest within stirs without delay.

Satyavan, as usual, readied himself well,
To carry the yoke, his daily toil to fulfill.
Unaware of fate, he set out with stride,
Bound to the rhythm of his daily guide.

"I shall join you on this day of my vow's end," she said,
But they declined, and still, she sped.
Following behind, her resolve unshaken,
"For the vow's sacred rule cannot be forsaken."

The princess, so delicate, soft, and refined,
Now treads the harsh forest paths aligned.
No longer a royal in palace grace,
She walks as a forester's wife in this place.

"Why come today, frail one, unbidden,
When rest for you was not forbidden?"
"The vow's sacred law," she softly replied,
"I have spoken of it dear; it cannot be denied."

"In the sweetness of your words, I yield,
O graceful maiden, my heart you've sealed.
I wish not to see you falter or stray,
Your triumph alone is my hope today."

"In life's journey, our victory's quest is mine," she said,
Her steadfast resolve in her heart was wed.
Unmoved by her words, though pure and clear,
The husband walked on, his wife held dear.

With blessings sought from her in-laws wise,
She stepped forth, resolve in her eyes.
As they walked, her husband would share,
The forest's beauty, its secrets laid bare.

Upon the earth, adorned in green,
The fawn lies nestled, serene,
The deer in graceful leaps do glide,
While cows and cuckoos in sweetness bide.

Satyavan gathered flowers and fruits with care,
Laying them gently, in order fair.
He reached for the wood, his task to fulfill,
Beside the tree, his hands poised still.

Toil has marked my brow with pain,
A burning heart I cannot sustain.
I cannot walk, nor stand, nor lie,
In sleep's calm embrace, I long to sigh.

Toil has bowed my head with pain,
A fiery heart I cannot sustain.
Neither can I walk, nor stand, nor stay,
In peaceful sleep, my solace lay.

Then she came, and knelt on the ground,
Her hands upon his brow, where rest was found.
She fanned him gently, soothing the air,
In devotion's grace, her heart laid bare.

Clad in garments stained with blood’s dark hue,
A figure shadowed, with fear anew.
In its grasp, the noose did bind,
And terror awoke within his mind.

Gently she placed Satyavan’s head down,
And rose with grace, her face renown.
With folded hands, to the radiant form,
She bowed and spoke, her plea most warm.

"Are you a deity?" she humbly inquired,
"What brings you here, and what is desired?
I seek the truth of your noble guise,
Forgive my questions, if they seem unwise."

"O pious one, steadfast in your vow,
To your question, my answer I offer now.
I am Yama, the lord of death's domain,
From the divine realms, so here I came."

"Your beloved's time on earth is done,
His life must cease, its course has run.
With the noose in hand, I've come today,
Bound by the path of duty's way."

"The laws of creation are firmly drawn,
Their course eternal, from dusk to dawn.
Few may grasp their intricate design,
But the wise discern their thread divine."

"The fate of mortals rests in my hand,
Their lives I claim by divine command.
Thus, I've come this very day,
To take the prince's soul away."

"Messengers of Time come to bind,
Mortal lives to fate aligned.
This truth I learned in childhood's day,
From elders' words and sages' way."

"O Lord of might, you've graced this place,
A marvel it is to behold your face.
Pray, reveal the reason you stand before me,
My yearning to know grows endlessly."

Seeing her curiosity, he softly spoke,
The lord of ancestors, his words bespoke:
"Handsome in form, in virtue profound,
He lived by dharma, with honour unbound."

He cherished his parents with tender care,
A beacon of compassion, beyond compare.
Speaking of the life that in him dwelled,
He drew it gently, as fate compelled."

The fire waned, the sacrifice ceased,
The body lay still, life released.
Yama, the lord, began his stride,
Towards the southern realms, his destined guide.

In sorrow and pain, the wife did tread,
Trailing behind, her heart full of dread.
Yet, to her, it seemed, as if by fate's weave,
Her husband's path was the one she must cleave.

Behind Him, the sound of footsteps came,
The law of time, unyielding in its claim.
For when man's time is marked to end,
No turning back, no chance to amend.

“Return to your home, where rites duties abide,
With future actions, fate will decide.
To fulfill your husband's debt is your way,
This, your task, your sacrcd stay.”

The virtuous one stood, answering the king's call,
In devotion unwavering, her heart stood tall.
When her husband moves, or bears his pain,
The wife follows, as is her sacred gain.

"With devotion alone, I tread this way,
Guided by dharma, come what may.
Thus, O Lord, I humbly implore,
Grant me the strength to speak once more."

"To walk seven steps together, they say,
Forms a bond of friendship that holds its sway.
With courage, I seek this sacred thread,
And offer these words with faith widespread."

"The husband is the wife's divine guide,
Where dharma dwells, there she'll abide.
What power, O Lord, could pull me away,
From dharma's call, where my heart must stay?"

"Two bodies we are, yet one soul we share,
Bound by love, a bond beyond compare.
Should that soul depart, its essence lost,
This body remains, an empty host."

"Though her words are firm, she is but young,
Judge not her heart by her fiery tongue.
Is it not dharma, O Lord, I pray,
For a wife to seek her husband's way?"

O Lord of Dharma," she humbly said,
"Guided by righteousness, these words I've spread.
Forgive me, divine one, for fate has decreed,
That courage and resolve are my only creed."

"Those crowned divine, with hearts of grace,
Show mercy to all, in every place.
You are a god, and I but mortal here,
Grant your compassion to this helpless dear."

Canto – VI

Journey Towards The Victory

Canto VI continues Savitri's remarkable journey of devotion, highlighting her eloquent dialogue with Yama, her committed faith, and the ultimate victory of her love and virtue over death. Through a series of boons, she artfully secures her husband's life and blessings for her family, ending in a joyous reunion with Satyavan.

Yama, impressed by Savitri's firm commitment and graceful words, offers her a series of boons. Her eloquence and faith move him to grant her requests, starting with restoring her father-in-law's kingdom and sight. Savitri also seeks blessings for children, ensuring the continuation of Satyavan's lineage.

Savitri firm in her resolve, follows Yama into the depths of his domain, refusing to leave her husband's side. Her arguments are rooted in dharma, marriage's sacred bond, and the souls' eternal unity.

Yama, though a deity, is enthralled by Savitri's wisdom and gentle persistence. Her words reflect her devotion and a profound understanding of dharma, virtue, and love.

Savitri's ultimate boon is her husband's life, which she secures with her profound argumentation and stanch dedication. Yama, moved by her devotion and moral strength, returns Satyavan's soul, granting them both a renewed life together.

After Yama departs, Savitri returns to Satyavan's lifeless body. With his soul restored, he awakens, and the two are joyously reunited. Their love, tested by fate, emerges stronger and blessed.

Canto VI embodies triumph and fulfilment. The tone shifts from tension and sorrow to admiration and celebration as Savitri's determination pays off. It emphasises, the power of love and devotion to overcome even the gravest obstacles, the beauty of dharma when upheld with faith and compassion and the transformative nature of virtue, which can influence even the cosmic laws of death.

Through Savitri, the canto exalts the ideals of moral strength, the sacred bond of marriage, and the divine justice inherent in unwavering faith.

"I cherish your graceful gait and tender words,
The splendour of your style, a beauty that accords.
When women of virtue walk this earth,
I proclaim the world is blessed with worth."

"Ask, O noble one, for a boon you desire,
A keeper of dharma, your soul inspires.
With your steadfast grace, life's path you weave,
Speak your wish, and now, I shall give."

"My father-in-law has lost his reign,
May his kingdom be his again.
Now blind, he dwells in this sacred space,
An ashram his shelter, a humble place."

"May his sight return, his valour rise,
Let the crown once more grace his skies.
O divine protector, heed my prayer,
Grant this boon, my heart lays bare," she declared.

"Thus, be it," he uttered, as he journeyed forth,
Towards the southern winds, unyielding in her course.
Without fear, she moved, the shadow of death to face,
Her heart unwavering, as she pursued her grace."

"Why should weariness find you here,
When I've granted wishes, hopes sincere?"
"With my life's breath bound to his side,
What weariness can daunt this love, this pride?"

"How can one bear the loss of him,
Whose hand once held, now lost to the dim?
"How can the body endure such strife,
When even the path of water cuts like life?"

"Two lives entwined, as fate's decree,
To walk together in marriage, bound yet free.
How can I walk this path alone,
O Lord of Dharma, King of the Throne?"

"Where shall thou lead my soul's true guide?
Where you tread, I walk by your side.
Is it the saints' embrace, those lights the way?
Shall I call upon their wisdom, as night turns to day?"

"I hold the truth, yet a child I stand,
In the realm of Dharma, at life's command.
Shall I seek my husband's blessing true?
O merciful Lord, my plea is for you."

"Your words, like the earth, bear weight and might,
Once more you ask, for a boon to alight.
Bearing my husband's life, a heavy toll,
I seek another's grace to make me whole."

"For the legacy of my father's line,
A childless void, where heirs should shine.
Grant, O Lord, your mercy's grace,
A progeny blessed, in your divine embrace."

"To nurture the clan, sons and daughters arise,
Growing strong beneath the vast, blessed skies.
By your grace, O Lord, my father shall see,
Joy and prosperity, his lineage set free."

"Enough of this toil and trek," Yama sighed,
"Far you've travelled, with none by your side.
The tender-footed one, through forests to tread,
Seems unfit to the world where mercy has fled."

In her husband's presence, no toil should she bear,
Yet the maiden falters, burdened by care.
Her weary form seeks solace and grace,
From the Lord of all, in this sacred space.

"Satyavan, my beloved, bears such strain,
I cannot endure his lingering pain.
To the realm where his journey shall lead,
I too shall follow, with love as my creed."

A youthful son, a hero you stand,
Praised by the wise across the land.
A King adept in Dharma's ways,
Devoted to his people's praise.

"The saint who walks on Dharma's Road,
Knows the path where virtue is sowed.
The company of saints, bears fruit divine,
Where joy prevails, no fear shall align."

The sacred tongue of Dharma's lore,
Brought joy to Yama's heart once more.
To the revered maiden, in devotion's grace,
He saw love and faith in her radiant face.

"Ask yet again, a boon I'll bestow,
For your words, like clouds, in beauty flow.
Your tender speech, with love entwined,
Enchants the heart, and calms the mind."

"Within my womb, Satyavan's heir,
Grant me, sons, with tender care.
Bestow your mercy, O Lord divine,
That in this birth, my soul may shine."

"In love's embrace, a child is born,
A boon from you, with grace adorned.
Let no shadow tread in my wake,
For all I've sought, in faith, I take."

The words of the righteous, the Sun star,
Lighting the world, no matter how far.
The saints' footsteps, serene and bright,
Glow as the beacon through endless night.

"Without my lord, I stray from the way,
Your words, though spoken, seem led astray.
Yet in my womb, a blessing takes flight—
Satyavan's line shall rise in the light."

"The boon you gave, now blooms anew,
To grant him life, as fate's due.
Behind his words, a truth unfolds,
A promise kept, as destiny holds."

"Had he not risen, the fault would be mine,
For Dharma's law would its judgment consign.
Yet with your grace, I gave my soul,
To life anew, in love's pure goal."

"O, the woman of Dharma, your touch so divine,
Freed your beloved from bondage's twine.
For four hundred years, life's sacred flame,
Burn bright with offerings in Yagna's name."

Yama blessed, "Let your deeds illuminate the world,
As the sun and moon in the sky are unfurled.
Those who understand Dharma's subtle grace,
Are blessed, living in this world's embrace."

Thus, he journeyed to the divine abode,
Bestowing blessings, in Dharma's code.
She, in sorrow, walked the path alone,
To where her Satyavan in rest was thrown.

Upon her lap, she rested his weary head,
Yet softly cried, her words unsaid.
From the depths of slumber, he softly rose,
And sat beside her, where solace flows.

Canto – VII

Satyavan's Return To Life

Canto VII presents the aftermath of Satyavan's return to life, the emotional reunion with his family, and the celebration of Savitri's extraordinary devotion and virtue. It reflects on the complexities of human emotions, the trials of life, and the triumph of faith and righteousness.

Satyavan, now alive, reflects on his ordeal with confusion and gratitude. He questions whether his experience was a dream or reality, as he feels the lingering effects of his journey to death and back. Savitri consoles him, encouraging him to rest and promising to reveal the full story at dawn.

The couple embarks on their journey back to the ashram. The forest, filled with shadows and sounds of wild beasts, mirrors the haunting fear and uncertainty of their experience. Yet, Savitri's resolve and love guide them forward, even as nature's grandeur and dangers loom large.

In the ashram, Satyavan's parents, Dyumatsena, and his wife, anxiously await their return. Dyumatsena's sight is miraculously restored, and he regains his physical and spiritual strength. The sages gather, their wisdom illuminating the sacred space, and they marvel at the unfolding events.

Upon their return, Satyavan's mother embraces him in tears, while his father stands silent, overwhelmed by emotion. The sages praise Savitri's strong devotion and admire her virtue, declaring her an inspiration of honour and grace.

The sages chant hymns and speak of Savitri's wisdom, courage, and dedication. They honour her as a paragon of dharma and a guiding light for all.

The canto delves into the nature of human life as a blend of joy and sorrow. It underscores the value of perseverance, faith, and love in overcoming life's trials.

Dyumatsena's restoration marks the symbolic triumph of righteousness and justice. His regained sight signifies clarity and hope for his lineage and kingdom.

Canto VII is both celebratory and contemplative, blending emotional intensity with philosophical depth. It celebrates Savitri's unshakable virtue and love while reflecting on the transient nature of life and the interplay of joy and sorrow, the transformative power of love and faith in overcoming adversity, and the role of dharma as a guiding principle for navigating life's challenges.

Savitri's story resonates as a timeless testament to the strength of the human spirit, the sanctity of love, and the profound impact of unwavering devotion.

"Where has the one I beheld now fled,
Leaving my heart in a restless dread?
Does your thigh now throb with pain?
Why then this pause, this lingering chain?"

"Is it dream or truth that holds me bound,
O dearest one, where answers are found?
If you know, then speak, let the veil part,
For longing consumes this restless heart."

"See, my dearest, night drapes the skies,
Shadows veil the world from our eyes.
The path is lost, you're weary, rest, be still,
Tomorrow, our tale, I promise, will spill."

The wild beasts cry, their echoes near,
Leaves rustle softly, trembling with fear.
Shadows of dread cast a haunting veil—
"Can this path be walked, or must we fail?"

The barren tree, its roots entwined,
A weary soul seeks solace, resigned.
Night fades away, lost in the dark,
Yet the journey calls, with the dawn's first spark.

"You, with your assent, stand apart,
Fit to end the night, the fading dark.
Before the sun breaks the dawn's embrace,
You are the fortune that guides the chase."

The head bears a pain, harsh and deep,
Yet life stirs within, where shadows sleep.
In the ashram, with dear and tender care,
Mothers nourish their young with love's prayer.

Our path is watched, both theirs and ours,
By those who stand, bound by their powers.
Time drifts away, silent, unspoken,
A mother's wisdom, quietly unbroken.

"I am the heir of a lineage deep,
Where thoughts of the past in silence sleep.
My mother grows frail, my father blind—
What am I, to them, in their tender mind?"

The sages near the hermit's gate,
Call and ask, in silence, fate.
"Is it not time, with haste and grace,
To tread towards the ashram's sacred place?"

"How long has time, like shadows, flown,
Beyond the grasp of my heart's lone throne?
Can the sorrow of their absence, deep,
Be borne by a soul, in silence, to weep?"

"Indeed, I too have felt the sting,
A pain as sharp as the wasp's wing.
I saw the weariness in your frame,
And so I spoke, in sorrow's name."

She walked, with her husband as guide,
Knowing the truth, her heart opens wide.
In the dark, shadows of fear did creep,
Yet still they moved, where silence sleeps.

The fear of Yama's path, like a child's dread,
Haunts the soul, where shadows are spread.
Yet in her, the virtues of penance and grace,
Shine through like an offering, a sacred trace.

The stone may stumble, the path may dip,
Such is the course where life's wheels slip.
The chariot of life, with strength to guide,
Moves forward, with fate as its steady stride.

Why does nature, in its grandeur vast,
Cause strife in man, a storm to last?
Yet, walking in harmony, hand in hand,
The path ahead leads to a goal so grand.

Where the love of parents dwells, pure and true,
The heart finds no solace, no refuge anew.
Unable to pause, nor to advance,
Caught between trials, in fate's cruel dance.

Having gained this human form, what is life but toil?
To walk together, enduring hardship's soil,
The lesson of life, through pain, is taught,
A journey of struggle, by fate's design wrought.

In a distant ashram, his father resides,
Dyumatsena's sight now opened wide.
A vision of joy in his heart does bring,
Yet the son's worry deepens a shadowed sting.

Joy and sorrow, entangled, both dwell,
A truth unknown to those who cannot tell.
Yet the wise, in self's true essence see,
The union of soul and thought, bound free.

As night fell, the daughter-in-law's heart was laden,
In search of her child, by worry overtaken.
With anxious care, she turned to her spouse,
Together they ventured, through the shadowed house

The sages, with attentive ears, did hear,
Driven by a longing, deep and clear.
The forest dwellers, in wonder, drew near,
Standing in awe, their hearts gripped by fear.

“Why worry, when Satyvan, surely returns,
With peace and grace, as wisdom burns?”
His wife, devoted to the path of light,
Walks in the shadow of virtue, pure and bright.

“Blessed are you and Satyvan who has such a wife,
In this world, a treasure beyond all strife.
For when she speaks, her words are wise,
Honoured by sages and revered in the skies.”

Dhaugmya, Gautama, Bharadwaja, and more,
Dalbhya, Aapastambha, whose wisdoms soar,
All the sages, in unison, spoke with grace,
Of virtue and truth, in a sacred embrace.

"Why this sorrow, when the wife's noble grace,
Illuminates life with virtue's embrace?"
A vision of fortune now comes to unfold,
Bringing peace, as the king's reign takes hold.

When the disciple called, with eager voice,
"Behold, the couple arrives," to all rejoice.
Seeing their coming, the banyan trees swayed,
In joyful dance, their branches played.

The mother, in sorrow, clasped her child tight,
Tears falling freely, her heart lost to the night.
The father stood still, speechless, withdrawn,
A mute witness to sorrow, as dawn met the dawn.

The sages, with fire, encircled in deep,
Their chants echoing, where shadows sleep.
"Why did the prince, through the quiet night,
Delay beyond time, when dawn's first light?"

Speak swiftly, what barrier has come to light?
For those who labour, love shines pure and bright. In the
face of hardship, love's true embrace,
Is seen in a child's care, a gentle grace.

The sons of Pandu, hearing the tale,
Forgot their sorrow as the story sailed.
Amidst the world's endless, shifting tide,
A woman’s honour stands, with grace and pride.

The lives of those gone serve as a light,
Guiding the path for those in the night.
The sage's sweet words, with voice so pure,
Brought life to the heart, a spirit to endure.

Canto – VIII

Conquest Of Death

Canto VIII concludes Savitri's epic journey, celebrating her courage, devotion, and the divine rewards that follow her unwavering commitment to dharma, love, and faith. It presents the resolution of her trials and the joyous restoration of her family's fortune and legacy.

Satyavan recounts his near-death experience, reflecting on the pain, his temporary rest, and the miraculous revival granted by Yama's grace. He acknowledges Savitri's role in his survival, attributing her wisdom, courage, and devotion to their ultimate accomplishment.

Sages such as Gautama and Narada recognise Savitri's divine nature and praise her understanding of truth and dharma. Her actions are hailed as an example of firm devotion and spiritual insight.

Through Savitri's resolve and the boons granted by Yama, her father-in-law Dyumatsena regains his sight and kingdom. The reconciliation of familial ties and the restoration of the lineage signify the triumph of righteousness and dharma.

The five boons symbolise Savitri's mastery over fate through her devotion and love. Her unwavering fast and prayer are celebrated as a testament to the power of faith and spiritual dedication.

The people of Salva and Madra rejoice in the restoration of peace and prosperity. The union of the two noble families becomes a beacon of harmony and virtue, inspiring all who hear their tale.

The canto highlights Dharma's transformative power and devotion's role in transcending human limitations. It highlights the virtues of courage, truth, and faith as the foundation of a meaningful life.

The canto concludes with a homage to Sage Vyasa, attributing the story's preservation to his wisdom and poetic mastery. The blessings of the tale are extended to readers, promising spiritual merit and joy to those who embrace its message.

The tone of Canto VIII is triumphant and celebratory, emphasizing the resolution of conflict and the restoration of harmony. It conveys profound messages such as Love and devotion are powerful forces capable of overcoming even death, Faith in dharma ensures justice and the ultimate triumph of righteousness. The legacy of such stories carries timeless lessons of hope, resilience, and virtue.

Savitri's tale concludes as a luminous example of the highest ideals of human conduct, leaving an indelible mark on the hearts of those who listen and learn.

"With my parents' blessing, I set my course,
Hand in hand with my love, a steady force,
As I took the axe to cleave the wood,
Time rushed ahead, as swift as it could."

“Unable to endure the pain in my head,
I rested upon my love's gentle bed,
For countless hours, in slumber deep I lay,
Awoke at last, with dawn's first light of day."

"The sage Gautama spoke with grace,
All wisdom lies within Savitri's face,
Truth is she bears, in her father's sight,
A hidden vision, veiled in light.”

"After long hours, she knew the cause,
A goddess in form, with regal laws,
Her wisdom vast, a sovereign's grace,
She held the keys to time and space."

"Truth, unhidden, without disguise,
In joyous company, it lies,
The sage Narada spoke with grace,
Your death awaits, but not in this place.”

"The day I spoke of death was past,
Yet now it lingers, thought to last.
With love's desire, I sought and won,
Beside my lord, I walked as one."

"To summon my lord, a vow I swore,
Seeking divine grace, my spirit bore.
To claim my husband's soul, as fate decreed,
Yama himself did answer the need."

"I beheld him, implored, and followed with care,
In mercy's light, he paused to spare.
To my stone-like heart, his grace did flow,
And granted the boon I dared to know."

"He granted my wish, yet with my lord gone,
Without his breath, life seemed withdrawn.
In his absence, I felt my existence was naught,
A great void, where meaning once was sought."

"My heart melted with steadfast devotion,
The life given to me now reaches its final motion.
Thus ended the vision, once full of dread,
Today, in the forest's heart, it has fled."

"With five boons in hand, I returned to stand,
Beside the divine man, in the heavenly land.
May the kingdom of sight, to my uncle, restore,
And swiftly may it be, as fate has in store."

"To claim my husband's life, a vow I kept,
Three days of fasting, in silence I wept.
By your divine grace, my soul is restored,
In this life of mine, your blessings poured."

"I cannot claim my victory, for the vow's glory shines,
In devotion to the divine, truth in life aligns.
When faith in the gods fills the heart of man,
Life, pure, as truth's eternal span."

"When the wife displayed her unwavering devotion,
All admired her, touched by her pure emotion.
With reverence, the Royal court did behold,
As sages, too, praised her heart of gold."

"May the lamp of your life shine ever bright,
And the glory of the devoted wife takes flight.
With thoughts of auspiciousness, we long to see,
The legacy as the lineage of eternity."

"The people of Salva's land arrived in haste,
To proclaim the victory of their king in great taste.
"You are our king,' they cried with devotion,
We've come to call you, with heartfelt emotion."

"Then the enemy king met his final end,
The gaze of the king upon him did bend.
Seeing this, with joy, they all took their leave,
Heading back to their land, as they did believe."

"Yama bestowed his breath, and all boons did unfold,
Granting their fruits, as destinies were told.
The people of Madra, Salva's land, in joy,
Rejoiced in peace, their hearts without alloy."

"Both noble lineages shone with life's bright glow,
In youth's pure heart, their virtues did flow.
The path of virtue, in friendship's embrace,
Echoed the song of a life of grace."

"Sage Vyasa, who wrote the tale of Mahabharat's lore,
Sung in verse by Chidambar, where truths ever soar.
To the hearts of connoisseurs who read with delight,
He offers his reverence, shining bright."

"May the sage's gaze bring blessings to all,
Conceding virtue and joy to answer the call.
Let the stream of poetry, pure and wide,
Sow seeds of merit, in which grace shall reside."

Bibliography & References

1. Chinmayanand Swami, *Kathop Upanishad,* Chinmaya Prakashan, New Delhi. 2018.
2. Swahananda Swami, *Chandogya Upanishad,* Sri Ramakrishna Math, New Delhi. 2009.
3. Hegade Srirang, Vyasa, *Mahabharata* (Translated into Kannada), P. C. Shabadimath Book Depot, Gadag, Karnataka.
4. Devdutt Pattanaik, *Garuda Purana and Other Hindu Ideas on Death, Rebirth and Immortality,* Westland, 25 Jul 2023.
5. Aurobindo, *Savitri (Fourth Edition)* Sri Aurobindo Ashram Publication, Pondichéry, 1993.
6. Kisari Mohan Ganguli, Translated Title "*The Mahabharata of Krishna-Dwaipayana Vyasa*" publisher Forgotten Books, 2018
7. Swami Prabhavananda and Christopher Isherwood, *Bhagavad Gita: The Song of God,* 2023.
8. Swami Sivananda, *"The Bhagavad Gita"* Publisher: The Divine Life Society, 2021.
9. (widely circulated PDF also available at sivanandaonline.org)
10. Swami Sarvananda, "Katha Upanishad", published by Sri Ramakrishna Math, 2002.